Original title:
Wishing on Dreamy Stars

Copyright © 2024 Creative Arts Management OÜ
All rights reserved.

Author: Matthew Whitaker
ISBN HARDBACK: 978-9916-90-400-8
ISBN PAPERBACK: 978-9916-90-401-5

Dancing in the Twilight of Hopes

In a world where shadows play,
Hopeful hearts find their way.
Stars whisper secrets in the night,
Guiding souls with gentle light.

We twirl beneath the fading sun,
In dreams of what we've yet to run.
With every spark that we ignite,
Our spirits soar in pure delight.

Embrace the dusk, let go of fear,
In this moment, we draw near.
With every step, we forge the path,
Light and laughter in our aftermath.

So dance along the twilight's edge,
In unity, we make our pledge.
For in this time, our hopes arise,
Together, we become the skies.

Murmurs in the Astral Breeze

In the silence of the night,
Stars hum softly, pure and bright.
Celestial whispers in the air,
Kissing dreams that we all share.

Galaxies spin, their tales unfold,
Tales of love and hearts so bold.
Each shimmer dances, wild and free,
An astral song calls out to me.

Beneath the moon's enchanting glow,
We find the truths we've come to know.
The universe, it breathes and sighs,
In every heartbeat, hope replies.

So listen close, hear the sweet sound,
In the breeze, our dreams are found.
For in this vast, eternal sea,
The murmurs guide our destiny.

Twilight Dreams and Cosmic Treasures

As twilight falls on quiet hills,
Soft dreams awaken, time stands still.
In the pastel hues of dusk,
We seek the treasures, bold and husk.

Cosmic wonders twinkle bright,
In the canvas of the night.
Stars like jewels, they intertwine,
In the vastness, we redefine.

Carried by the evening's grace,
We find our fortitude, our place.
With open hearts and endless skies,
Twilight whispers, and hope replies.

So gather close, let spirits soar,
In this twilight, there's so much more.
With cosmic kisses, we'll explore,
In dreams, we are forevermore.

Nighttime Reflections of a Shimmering Future

In the quiet of the night,
We ponder futures, shining bright.
Reflections dance on starlit seas,
Promises carried on the breeze.

Each moment, a gem waiting to shine,
Time weaves stories, yours and mine.
Underneath the moon's soft gaze,
We craft our dreams in gentle ways.

With every thought, a pathway made,
In twilight's glow, our fears allayed.
For in the night, we mold desire,
And set our hearts and hopes afire.

So let us savor nighttime's grace,
In reflections, we find our place.
For in this shimmer, futures gleam,
Together we'll live out the dream.

A Symphony of Celestial Lights

In the vast expanse of night,
Stars twinkle bright with delight.
A dance of colors, a cosmic show,
Whispers of secrets only they know.

Each glow a note in heaven's song,
Harmonies where we all belong.
The universe sings of love unbound,
In the silence, beauty is found.

Embracing the Night's Embrace

Moonlight bathes the world in dreams,
Soft shadows stir like gentle streams.
Whispers echo through the trees,
Night wraps us up like a tender breeze.

Stars above weave tales so bright,
Every heartbeat feels just right.
In the stillness, hearts align,
Embracing night, our souls entwine.

Starlight Serenades of Hope

A lullaby sung by the stars,
Guiding lost souls from afar.
Hope glimmers in the midnight skies,
As dreams take flight, like birds that rise.

With every twinkle, a wish is made,
In the quiet night, fears will fade.
Together we soar on beams of light,
In starlit serenades, futures bright.

Dreams Carved in Silver Skies

In silver skies, our dreams take form,
Shaped by the twilight, soft and warm.
Every desire painted bold,
In hues of twilight, stories told.

With wings of light, we chase the dawn,
Each moment cherished, never gone.
Through the vastness, our spirits fly,
In the canvas of stars, we reside high.

Stardust Reveries

In whispers soft, the stardust glows,
A dance of light where wonder flows.
Beneath the night, our dreams take flight,
In silver threads, we find our sight.

Each twinkle hides a story spun,
Of cosmic tales, of worlds begun.
As we drift, the heavens call,
In stardust dreams, we rise and fall.

With every spark, a wish is cast,
In endless skies, our hopes amassed.
Through velvet dark, we journey far,
On wings of light, beneath a star.

So close your eyes and feel the breeze,
Let go the world, with tranquil ease.
In stardust reveries, we unite,
Bound by the magic of the night.

When the Sky Sings

When the sky sings, the world awakes,
With melodies that dance like lakes.
A symphony of clouds unfurled,
In gentle notes, reclaims the world.

The sun dips low, a golden hue,
As evening's tune begins anew.
Each star a note, each moonbeam bright,
Compose the dreams that fill the night.

With every breeze, a soft refrain,
A lullaby that holds our pain.
In harmony, our hearts entwined,
In sky's embrace, the soul refined.

So listen close, to nature's hum,
As twilight whispers, peace will come.
When the sky sings, we find our place,
In every note, a warm embrace.

Echoes of the Dreamscape

In shadows deep, the echoes play,
Through winding paths, where dreamers stray.
A canvas vast, of fears and joys,
In silent realms, both girls and boys.

Whispered thoughts like fireflies glow,
Illuminate the way we go.
In twilight hours, we find the key,
Unlocking doors to fantasy.

With gentle hands, the night bestows,
The magic in the way it flows.
Each echo calls, a voice divine,
In dreamscape's grasp, our hearts align.

So drift away on starlit beams,
Embrace the world that's born of dreams.
In echoes soft, our spirits soar,
Beyond the veil, forevermore.

Celestial Fantasies

In realms where time and space collide,
Celestial fantasies abide.
Where dreams are cast in cosmic light,
And every heart dares to take flight.

With planets swirling in a dance,
We reach for stars, we dare romance.
In celestial nights, our spirits glide,
On beams of hope, we trust the tide.

With galaxies that swirl like wine,
In astral hues, our souls align.
Through nebulae, where silence reigns,
We find our peace, release our chains.

So join the stars, embrace the night,
In fantasies born from pure delight.
Together we'll weave a tale so bright,
In celestial realms, we'll find our light.

Fables Under a Canopy of Stars

In the night, stories weave,
Whispers beneath bright lights.
Crickets play their soft tune,
As we dream of distant flights.

Tales of heroes lost and found,
Echo softly through the trees.
Each twinkle holds a secret,
Carried upon the evening breeze.

Beneath this vast and wondrous sky,
Imagination takes its flight.
Fables linger in the air,
As we bask in the moonlight.

Heavenly Reflections of Us

In mirrors of the endless night,
We see our hearts dance and gleam.
Reflections of love shine bright,
Captured in a soft moonbeam.

Stars align, guiding our way,
With dreams that sparkle like the sea.
Hand in hand, we choose to stay,
In a world just you and me.

Every moment, a cherished glance,
Underneath this cosmic glow.
Together, we take our chance,
In the light of stars that flow.

Map of Dreams Under the Moon

Upon the canvas of the night,
Dreams are drawn with silver thread.
The moon sketches our delight,
With paths of light where we are led.

Each star a marker of our fate,
Guiding us through the unknown.
In this vast, celestial state,
Our hopes and wishes have grown.

We traverse the skies so wide,
With hearts open to the call.
Together, we dream and glide,
As starlit dreams fill our thrall.

Cosmic Reflections in Midnight Waters

In the stillness, waters gleam,
Reflecting stars that softly sway.
Whispers of an ancient dream,
Guide us through the dark ballet.

The cosmos dances in the deep,
Rippling with echoes of the past.
Secrets in the silence keep,
Moments fleeting yet steadfast.

Hand in hand, we lean and gaze,
At the universe's sweet embrace.
In this cosmic, watery haze,
We find our ever-cherished place.

Light Trails of Forgotten Hopes

In twilight's grasp, we chase the gleams,
Faded dreams still whisper through the seams.
A spark ignites in shadows deep,
Where forgotten hopes begin to creep.

Stars align and guide the way,
To light the paths that lead astray.
In every flicker, stories dwell,
Of silent wishes cast like spells.

We gather light from fading days,
In the silence, hope still stays.
With every step, the darkness bends,
As light trails form, my heart ascends.

In the night's embrace, we find our song,
A melody of where we belong.
With every breath, the echoes flow,
Through light trails of forgotten hope's glow.

Beyond the Cosmic Canvas

Beneath the stars, we dream anew,
Infinite colors in shades of blue.
Each brushstroke paints a tale so bright,
Beyond the cosmic canvas of night.

Galaxies swirl in a timeless dance,
Whispers of fate in a fleeting glance.
A universe filled with tales untold,
In every shadow, a heart of gold.

Nebulae bloom in vibrant hues,
Awakening thoughts and cherished views.
Beyond the edges of what we know,
A tapestry of hope begins to flow.

As constellations weave their thread,
In cosmic grandeur, we are led.
To realms where dreams and starlight blend,
Beyond the canvas, hopes transcend.

Hopes Illuminated by the Cosmos

In the vastness of the night sky,
Echoes of dreams begin to fly.
Each twinkling star, a wish set free,
Hopes illuminated, wild as the sea.

With every pulse of distant light,
We gather strength to face the night.
A galaxy of hopes collide,
In cosmic realms where dreams abide.

Through stellar storms and silent rays,
We find the spark that brightly stays.
In constellations, stories weave,
From hopes illuminated, we believe.

As moons rise high and shadows fade,
In the cosmos' glow, we are made.
Boundless visions dance in space,
Hopes illuminated, we embrace.

Night Blossoms of Hope and Wonder

In the garden where shadows play,
Night blossoms bloom, and dreams display.
Petals whisper secrets of the heart,
In every moment, magic's part.

A gentle breeze stirs the night air,
As stars adorn the landscape rare.
In the silence, wishes softly stir,
Night's embrace makes our spirits purr.

With every twinkle, stories grow,
In moonlit gardens, hopes do flow.
Each flower opens to reveal,
The wonder that the dark can heal.

In twilight's arms, we find our place,
Amid night blossoms, hopes interlace.
With every breath, new dreams unfurl,
In the wonder of this twilight world.

Dreamcatchers of the Night

In shadows deep, they weave and bind,
A net of stars to catch the dreams.
Whispers float on silken threads,
While moonlight dances, softly gleams.

Each wish held tight, a secret shared,
With every breath, the night unfolds.
The dreams, like butterflies, take flight,
In gentle hands, their stories told.

Underneath the vast expanse,
The dreamers find their solace bright.
With hope entwined in every glance,
They chase the magic of the night.

In the stillness, dreams revive,
Awakening the heart's delight.
Together, as the stars all thrive,
They whisper secrets, pure and light.

Wishes in the Milky Way

A galaxy of dreams alight,
Where wishes flow like cosmic streams.
In stardust paths, our hearts take flight,
Embracing hope, igniting dreams.

With every twinkle, secrets soar,
A moment caught in timeless space.
Each whisper lights the universe,
A dance of wonder, grace, and grace.

Through velvet skies, the wishes glide,
Past swirling hues of blue and gold.
They travel far, a cosmic ride,
In searching hearts, their tales unfold.

Oh, to be lost where stars align,
In dreams we're free, where wishes play.
Together, we will brightly shine,
As love will guide our souls away.

A Tapestry of Light

Threads of silver weave the night,
In patterns danced by cosmic arms.
Each stitch a story, soft and bright,
A tapestry of nature's charms.

The colors blend, a vibrant hue,
Where every star a note of grace.
In every heart, the warmth shines through,
A symphony in endless space.

With every glance, new dreams are spun,
In woven tales of hope and fire.
As morning breaks, the stars are done,
But night returns, igniting desire.

So let us craft this wondrous art,
Together, in the softest night.
For in each thread, we find our part,
In every soul, a spark of light.

Heartbeats among the Nebulae

In swirling clouds of vibrant hues,
The heartbeats pulse with cosmic grace.
Each thump a note in vast parades,
A rhythm found in boundless space.

The nebulae hum a lullaby,
Where dreams take form in gentle sways.
With whispers lost, they drift and fly,
In tender arms of endless days.

Each heartbeat maps a journey wide,
In starlit trails, our paths entwine.
We chase the echoes, side by side,
In universe, where hearts align.

So dance with me through cosmic night,
In every pulse, we find our way.
Together, we'll embrace the light,
Among the stars, we'll always stay.

Chasing Celestial Echoes

Beneath the vast and starry skies,
We chase the whispers of our fate,
Each echo sings of long-lost dreams,
In twilight's arms, we hesitate.

The moonlight dances on the sea,
With silver trails of ancient tales,
As hearts entwine in cosmic flight,
We sail on hope, where starlight fails.

Through shadows dark, our spirits rise,
To meet the dawn with hopeful grace,
In every heartbeat, endless sighs,
We find our truth in empty space.

So let us chase these echoes bright,
And paint our dreams on heaven's chest,
For in the glow of each soft light,
We find our path, we find our rest.

Aurora of Desires

Across the hills, the sky ignites,
With hues of pink and golden glow,
Awakening the world in dreams,
A dance of light, a fervent show.

Where shadows blend with morning's grace,
Our wishes float on gentle breeze,
In every stroke, a soft embrace,
The dawn whispers, "Just believe."

Beneath the arc of waking light,
We gather hopes, both old and new,
In every breath, a wish takes flight,
As sunlight bathes the world in hue.

This aurora of our desires,
Will guide us through the day ahead,
With every pulse, our hearts aspire,
To chase the dreams that love has bred.

Dreams Adrift in Stardust

In dreams, we wander, lost in time,
Adrift within a sea of stars,
Each thought a vessel, sleek and fine,
We sail the night, embrace our scars.

The cosmos breathes, a lullaby,
As stardust weaves through every sigh,
We dance beneath the endless sky,
In whispered hopes, our spirits fly.

With every twinkle, fate appears,
A promise wrapped in silver light,
Together we shall cast our fears,
And bathe in dreams that feel so right.

For in this space, we're free to roam,
A tapestry of hearts combined,
Adrift in stardust, we are home,
A universe of love designed.

Twinkling Promises of the Night

The stars are scattered across the night,
A blanket woven with dreams untold,
Each twinkle holds a promise bright,
A story waiting to unfold.

In this vast expanse, we find our way,
With whispered vows that time can't sever,
Together under skies of gray,
We chase the moments, lost forever.

The moon, a guide through shadows deep,
Illuminates the paths we take,
As secrets of the night we keep,
With every step, our hearts awake.

So let us dance beneath this dome,
With dreams alight like shimmering seas,
In twinkling promises, we roam,
Together, finding peace with ease.

Floating on Lunar Dreams

In the night, I drift away,
Softly guided by the sway.
Moonlit paths beneath my feet,
Where shadows and starlight meet.

Whispers dance upon the breeze,
Carrying tales of forgotten seas.
Each wave a shimmer, pure and bright,
Cradled gently by the night.

Stars like jewels, they twinkle low,
Inviting me to dance and flow.
In this realm where wishes gleam,
I find my heart in lunar dream.

Among the clouds, I softly soar,
Chasing echoes, wanting more.
In this space of silver gleam,
Forever lost in lunar dream.

Chasing the Aurora's Glow

Colors swirl in the midnight sky,
Dancing flames, they leap and fly.
Nature's brush with vibrant hue,
Painting dreams in shades anew.

Underneath the shimmering veil,
Adventurous hearts set to sail.
Each flicker, a promise untold,
In the magic, we find bold.

Whispers of the universe call,
In echoes soft, we rise and fall.
Wrapped in warmth, the night unveils,
The beauty held in nature's tales.

As dawn approaches, colors fade,
Leaving us with memories made.
In our hearts, the glow will stay,
Chasing light, come what may.

Enchanted by Celestial Whispers

In twilight's hush, I hear the song,
Of cosmic dreams where we belong.
Stars conspire in silent grace,
Calling souls to this sacred place.

Galaxies twirl like dancers bold,
In stories of the night foretold.
With every breath, I feel the change,
The universe in its vast range.

Comets trace their fiery trails,
Bearing secrets in their sails.
As echoes of the past resound,
In space and time, we are unbound.

Lost in wonder, I ascend,
To realms where dreams and stardust blend.
In this dance of light and sound,
Celestial whispers all around.

The Universe's Embrace

In the cradle of the night sky,
The universe breathes, oh so high.
Stars like diamonds softly gleam,
Within the fabric of a dream.

Galactic wonders, vast and wide,
Carrying secrets we confide.
Beneath the waves of cosmic flow,
We find our hearts in ebb and glow.

Nebulas weave their colorful threads,
Whispers of the past, though long dead.
In this embrace, we seek to know,
The depths of love that stars bestow.

As stardust settles on our skin,
The universe bids us to begin.
In this vastness, we find our place,
Forever held in the universe's embrace.

Lanterns of Hope

In the night, they softly glow,
Guiding hearts through shadows low.
Each flicker tells a story bright,
A beacon shining with pure light.

Amidst the dark, they hold the flame,
Whispering softly, calling names.
With every hue, they weave a dream,
In this vast world, we find our theme.

Together we walk, hand in hand,
Under the glow, we take a stand.
With lanterns raised, we touch the sky,
In unity, our spirits fly.

Cosmic Serenades

In the quiet of the starry night,
Whispers drift in endless flight.
Galaxies sing a gentle tune,
Beneath the gaze of the silver moon.

Nebulae dance with colors bold,
Tales of the cosmos waiting to unfold.
Each note wrapped in the vast unknown,
In harmony, we find our own.

Planets align in celestial sway,
Guiding dreamers who dare to play.
With every star, a wish is spun,
In the melody, we are all one.

The Light That Beckons

In the distance, a glow appears,
Drawing close, it calms our fears.
A gentle light that warms the soul,
Inviting us to lose control.

It dances across the night's expanse,
A shimmering flame in a cosmic dance.
With open hearts, we follow near,
Towards the promise, the light we hear.

With each step, shadows fade away,
In the brightness, we long to stay.
This guiding star, it leads us on,
To a place where hope is born.

Stars that Whisper Secrets

Beneath the night, they softly speak,
In murmurs low, their voices meek.
Each glimmer holds a tale untold,
A map of dreams in silver and gold.

Through velvet skies, their secrets weave,
With every twinkle, they gently leave.
Messages carried on the breeze,
Unlocking hearts and setting them free.

In starlit paths, we seek the truth,
Guided by innocence of youth.
What lies beyond, we yearn to know,
As stars watch over, softly aglow.

Stardust Wishes on a Celestial Highway

On a path where dreams ignite,
Stars whisper secrets in the night.
Wishes woven in the sky,
Dance like fireflies passing by.

Galaxies spin in vast embrace,
Chasing echoes through time and space.
Floating on a comet's tail,
Every heartbeat tells a tale.

Cosmic winds carry our hopes,
Traveling through the universe's slopes.
Radiant pathways made of light,
Guide us gently into the night.

In the quiet, stardust falls,
Painting wishes on cosmic walls.
Upon this highway, we align,
Boundless adventures, yours and mine.

Echoes of Distant Galaxies

In shadows cast by ancient stars,
Echoes of worlds that drift afar.
Silent whispers on the breeze,
Telling tales that never cease.

Light years travel through the void,
Memories linger, time enjoyed.
Constellations weave their dance,
In the silence, we find chance.

Fading light from long ago,
Guides our hearts, ignites the glow.
A canvas vast, the sky unfolds,
With every echo, a story told.

As we wander through the night,
Distant galaxies take flight.
Holding dreams that never fade,
In their beauty, hopes are laid.

Magical Trails of Shimmering Lights

Underneath a velvet sky,
Trails of light begin to fly.
Magic dust in moonlit streams,
Carrying softly our wild dreams.

Meteors streak like wishes thrown,
In silence, the universe has grown.
Each star a tale, bright and bold,
Stories waiting to be told.

Beyond the realms of time and space,
Shimmering lights greet us with grace.
A cosmic dance, ethereal hue,
Guiding us to realms anew.

In this journey, hand in hand,
We explore a starry land.
Magical trails will be our guide,
In the night, we'll gently glide.

Celestial Fantasies in the Horizon

At dawn, the colors rise and play,
Celestial fantasies greet the day.
Horizons bloom with shades so bright,
Painting whispers of morning light.

Planets spin in the azure dome,
Each a guardian, calling us home.
Voices echo from far and wide,
In the cosmos, we reside.

As the sun begins to soar,
Dreams awaken, forevermore.
Mysteries wrapped in morning haze,
Guide our hearts through endless ways.

With each moment, we will trust,
In celestial wonders and cosmic dust.
Fantasies in the horizon gleam,
Together we'll weave our shared dream.

Beneath the Veil of Infinity

In shadows deep, the cosmos calls,
Whispers float through silent halls.
Stars ignite a distant spark,
Guiding souls against the dark.

Waves of time in destined flow,
Secrets held in starlit glow.
Beneath the vast, eternal sky,
Dreamers rise and learn to fly.

Threads of fate entwine with light,
Chasing echoes of the night.
Lost in wonder, hearts align,
Beneath this veil, the stars define.

Across the dark, the galaxies spin,
Each new dawn, a chance to begin.
In the quiet, hopes take flight,
Beneath the veil, we find our light.

Starlit Pathways to Tomorrow

Upon the path where starlight beams,
Hope is sewn into our dreams.
Each step forward, futures weave,
In silver threads, we dare believe.

Through twilight's calm, a song will rise,
As constellations paint the skies.
Echoes of tomorrow's grace,
Guide us through this timeless space.

With every heartbeat, shadows part,
Illuminated by the art.
We walk the road of light and air,
In starlit whispers everywhere.

So let us chase the glowing dawn,
With spirits free, we will move on.
For every step is ours to claim,
On starlit pathways, we are the flame.

Celestial Whispers

In the quiet of the night,
Celestial whispers take their flight.
Voices soft as moonlit mist,
Calling forth what dreams persist.

From distant realms, the stories stream,
Painting skies with cosmic dreams.
As stars align, our hearts will sing,
To the tune the universe brings.

Drifting through this grand ballet,
Every thought finds its own way.
Secrets dwell in the twilight's embrace,
Whispers echo through time and space.

Let every spark illuminate,
The path to worlds that lie in wait.
In this silence, we shall find,
Celestial whispers, hearts entwined.

Starlit Aspirations

With eyes cast up, our souls ignite,
Chasing dreams into the night.
Each star a wish yet to unfold,
Stories waiting to be told.

From the depths of cosmic lore,
Visions bloom forevermore.
In the starlit dance, we rise,
Reaching out toward endless skies.

Guided by the north star's gleam,
We build our fate upon a dream.
Every heartbeat aligns with grace,
In this vast and timeless space.

So let us strive with hearts ablaze,
To seize the night and claim our days.
As starlit aspirations soar,
We find our truth forevermore.

Finding Ourselves Among the Stars

Under the vast celestial dome,
We wander, lost yet found,
Each twinkle echoes tales untold,
In dreams, our souls are unbound.

We reach for lights that seem so near,
Whispers of hope in the night,
Guiding us through endless space,
In our hearts, we ignite.

Every glance up ignites a flame,
A spark of the great unknown,
In starlit paths, we draw our names,
In the cosmos, we have grown.

Together we chase the starlit glow,
Mapping the universe's heart,
For in the dark, our answers flow,
Finding ourselves is the art.

Stardust Traces in the Night's Embrace

Whispers of stardust fill the air,
As shadows dance in swirling light,
We chase the dreams that linger near,
In the soft embrace of night.

Moments sparkle like tiny stars,
Fleeting, yet forever bright,
Each trace a memory from afar,
In the calm of the twilight.

Heartbeats sync with the cosmos' pulse,
In silence, our souls intertwine,
Through cosmic silk, we feel the result,
Of dreams and stars that align.

Under the moon's tender gaze,
We create magic, hand in hand,
In stardust, we'll forever blaze,
Among the glimmers, we stand.

Boundless Horizons of Aspiration

Beyond the mountains, dreams take flight,
In every heart, a spark ignites,
We reach for peaks beyond our sight,
With every dawn, new heights in sight.

Horizons stretch where visions grow,
Unseen paths beckon us to dare,
Each step we take, a river's flow,
Aspiration filled with care.

Together we'll rewrite our fate,
In the tapestry of the sky,
For each endeavor we create,
Is a whisper of dreams that fly.

With boundless hopes, we chart our course,
Navigating through the vast unknown,
In every heartbeat, find the source,
Of dreams we've claimed as our own.

Pathways Paved with Starlight

In the quiet of the unfolding night,
Pathways glow beneath the stars,
Guiding footsteps, soft and light,
Leading us through our memoirs.

Each twinkling orb a story spun,
Of journeys past, of love and loss,
In darkness, hope's whispers run,
Reminding us of the cost.

With every step, we find our place,
These paths of light, they softly show,
That in the vast and endless space,
We're never lost, only aglow.

Together, we walk this starlit way,
With hearts aligned, we chase the dawn,
Paved with dreams that will not sway,
In starlight, we are reborn.

Whispers of Celestial Desire

In twilight's hush, dreams softly tread,
Stars align as wishes are spread.
Moonlight dances on the sea,
Whispers of fate call out to me.

Galaxies spin in endless flight,
Hearts entwined in cosmic light.
Echoes linger in the still,
Yearning souls with dreams to fulfill.

In the silence, secrets bloom,
Cradled softly in the gloom.
Eternal jest of love's sweet game,
Awakens hearts, ignites the flame.

Together we drift, lost in the night,
Stars will guide us, our hearts unite.
In this realm of endless sighs,
Whispers hold our celestial ties.

Beneath the Glittering Veil

Under the sky where wishes soar,
Magic lingers, forevermore.
Each star a tale, a wish, a dream,
Beneath the veil, the cosmos gleam.

The moon sings softly to the night,
Casting shadows, weaving light.
Secrets hidden among the stars,
Fleeting moments, healed old scars.

A tapestry of fate is spun,
Threads of starlight, two become one.
The universe sways in soothing rhymes,
Beneath the veil, lost in time.

In every glance, the heavens sigh,
As dreams awaken, spirits fly.
In the quiet, our hopes reveal,
Together we stand, beneath the veil.

Night's Secret Promise

The night unfolds in whispers low,
Secrets woven in moonlit glow.
Stars fall silent, hearts align,
In this moment, love is divine.

A promise made beneath the sky,
In tender whispers, we draw nigh.
With every pulse, the shadows dance,
In the dark, we take our chance.

The world recedes, it's you and me,
Bound by fate, eternally free.
Gentle breezes carry our dreams,
In night's embrace, nothing's as it seems.

Let starlight guide us through the dark,
In every heartbeat, we leave a mark.
Night's embrace will never sever,
In secret promises, we endeavor.

Lullabies from the Cosmos

Stars above sing lullabies sweet,
A cosmic serenade, our hearts meet.
Galaxies sway, in rhythm and rhyme,
Time stands still, a moment sublime.

In gentle echoes, the universe sighs,
A symphony played where silence lies.
Each note a wish, a whispering dream,
Wrapped in stardust, a celestial theme.

With every breath, the cosmos seems near,
Cradling souls through the cosmic sphere.
As constellations paint tales so bright,
We find our peace in the endless night.

So heed the call, let worries flee,
In cosmic arms, forever be.
Lullabies weave through the endless skies,
In this vastness, our spirits rise.

Echoes from the Land of Stars

In whispers soft as twilight's breath,
Ancient tales of cosmic depth.
Where dreams take flight on starlit streams,
And time dissolves in endless themes.

Galaxies twirl like dancers bright,
Painting secrets in the night.
Each echo fades, yet lingers still,
A silent promise to fulfill.

Through nebulas that softly glow,
Unseen paths of light we know.
In every heart, a spark awaits,
To join the dance, to open gates.

So let us reach beyond the veil,
And let our spirits set the sail.
For in the vast, the echoes call,
A symphony that binds us all.

Stargazing for Lost Dreams

Under the blanket of the night,
We seek the stars, our guiding light.
In silence, hopes begin to bloom,
From shadows cast in quiet gloom.

Each twinkle holds a dream once kept,
In distant realms where wishes slept.
With every glance, we find our way,
To skies where fading visions play.

The constellations whisper truths,
Of youthful hearts and lost pursuits.
With open eyes and minds anew,
We trace the paths of what we knew.

For every star, a memory shines,
Illuminating future designs.
In stargazing, our spirits soar,
Reviving dreams forevermore.

Celestial Gardens of the Soul

In gardens where the starlight spills,
Awake the heart with whispered thrills.
Each petal glows with cosmic grace,
Reflecting light in time and space.

Galactic blooms in vibrant hues,
Awaken long-forgotten views.
With every breath, the magic flows,
As curiosity bestows.

In this embrace of night divine,
We feel the pulse of stars align.
The universe, a sacred scroll,
Unfolds the tale of each lost soul.

So let us wander, hand in hand,
Through celestial dreams so grand.
For in these gardens, we shall find,
The seeds of hope intertwined.

Ocean of Stars in the Night Sky

Beneath the waves of midnight blue,
An ocean of stars awaits anew.
Each shimmering point a story told,
Of ancient worlds, both young and old.

Waves of light that ebb and flow,
Carrying dreams where wishes go.
In this vast sea, we navigate,
Through constellations, we create.

The tide of time pulls us near,
To discover truths, crystal clear.
As starlit whispers kiss our skin,
We dive into the depths within.

So let us drift on cosmic seas,
Embracing calm, embracing peace.
For in this ocean, we are found,
Connected by the starlight's sound.

Nighttime Yearnings

In the hush of night, I sigh,
Stars whisper secrets, drifting by.
Moonlight spills on dreams untold,
A heart's desire, brave and bold.

Shadows dance in silver glow,
Beneath a canvas vast and slow.
Each twinkle echoes soft and clear,
Guiding wishes, drawing near.

Dreams in Cosmic Ink

Across the dark, we sketch our fate,
In cosmic ink, we contemplate.
Galaxies swirl, stories unfold,
Timeless tales of the brave and bold.

Nebulas paint the skies so bright,
Illuminating paths through the night.
In dreams, we soar, we dive, we spin,
Finding solace where hopes begin.

Glittering Hopes Above

Up in the sky, hopes glitter and shine,
Each star a wish, a longing divine.
With every spark, a heart beats free,
In endless night, we yearn to be.

Constellations weave our fate,
In stardust wrapped, we meditate.
Each flicker tells of journeys grand,
Together, we dream, hand in hand.

Beneath the Astral Veil

Beneath the veil of night's embrace,
Whispers linger in sacred space.
We wander paths of light and shade,
In cosmic realms, our dreams cascade.

Among the stars, our spirits roam,
Finding peace in the celestial dome.
Each breath a verse, a timeless song,
In the heart of night, we all belong.

The Elysium of Cosmic Aspirations

In the realm where stars ignite,
Dreams are born in endless flight.
Galaxies twist in radiant grace,
Time stands still in this sacred space.

Hearts unite like constellations,
Fueling hopes with bright foundations.
We dance upon the milky tide,
In Elysium, where wishes abide.

Whispers echo through the void,
Secrets of the cosmos enjoyed.
Here, ambitions find their wings,
And life begins in cosmic springs.

Through cosmic paths our spirits soar,
Chasing dreams forevermore.
In this realm, we rise and dive,
In aspirations, we come alive.

Wishes Cradled in Cosmic Light

In the cradle of a starry night,
Wishes take their gentle flight.
Softly glimmering, they weave and spin,
Guided by the dreams within.

Celestial voices serenade,
Echoing promises, never to fade.
Underneath the cosmic dome,
In this light, we find our home.

Each glance at the night sky,
Fills our hearts, makes spirits fly.
Holding wishes in our hands,
We craft our fate from stardust strands.

Through the darkness, hope ignites,
Carried on the wings of flights.
In every shimmer, a world so bright,
Our wishes cradle in cosmic light.

Dreamscapes Beneath an Astral Sea

Beneath the waves of azure night,
Dreamscapes dance in soft moonlight.
Rippling thoughts in endless flow,
Where secrets of the cosmos grow.

Stars like fish in shimmering trails,
Whispering tales of timeless sails.
In this sea, we drift and glide,
Caught in currents where dreams reside.

Galaxies bloom in vibrant hues,
Painting skies with midnight blues.
In the depths, our wishes swell,
A universe we long to tell.

Together we explore this sea,
Where every wave ignites, sets free.
In dreamscapes' arms, our hearts align,
Beneath the stars, our souls entwine.

Sails Beyond the Shimmering Veil

Set the sails for distant shores,
Where dreams await and freedom roars.
Beyond the veil of azure light,
We journey forth into the night.

Starlit winds guide our course,
With every wave, we find our force.
Through cosmic seas, we navigate,
Our hearts aligned with destiny's fate.

Whispers of the cosmos call,
Inviting us to rise and fall.
In every splash, a tale unfolds,
Of hopes and dreams like precious gold.

In the embrace of the infinite sky,
We sail with courage, let spirits fly.
To shores unknown we gladly sail,
Beyond the stars, beyond the veil.

Journey Through the Astral Lights

Stars whisper tales of dreams untold,
Each spark a story in the night sky bold.
We sail through galaxies, vast and bright,
Chasing the beams of shimmering light.

The cosmos wraps us in a velvet hug,
With every heartbeat, we feel the tug.
Through nebulae and comets' tails we glide,
In this astral dance, we shall abide.

Phoenixes Rising from Stardust

From ashes of night, they rise anew,
Feathers of fire, painted in hues.
With wings outstretched to embrace the dawn,
They soar through skies, reborn and drawn.

Each flame a promise, each flight a dream,
Through trials and turmoil, they find their gleam.
In the heart of darkness, they ignite the spark,
Phoenixes rising from the celestial dark.

Chronicles of Light and Longing

In the stillness of twilight, secrets unfold,
Stories of longing, both gentle and bold.
The moonlight whispers, guiding the way,
As hearts entwine under stars that sway.

Echoes of laughter dance on the breeze,
In the tapestry of night, we find our peace.
Each flickering star writes a line in the sand,
Chronicles of love, a celestial band.

Celestial Secrets in the Night

The night holds secrets, ancient and wise,
Beneath the vast canvas of starlit skies.
Dreams hidden softly in the folds of dark,
Celestial whispers leave their mark.

We wander through shadows, seeking the light,
In the arms of the universe, everything feels right.
With every heartbeat, with every sigh,
We uncover the truths as time drifts by.

Beneath the Twilight Canopy

The stars awaken, soft and bright,
Whispers of dusk, a gentle sight.
Shadows dance on emerald leaves,
Nature sighs, as daylight grieves.

Crickets sing their evening song,
In this world where dreams belong.
Moonbeams kiss the forest floor,
Secrets linger, forevermore.

A breeze carries stories untold,
Of ancient nights and hearts of gold.
Underneath the sky's embrace,
We find our hopes, our sacred space.

Together, we await the dawn,
In twilight's grasp, our spirits drawn.
Beneath this canopy of dreams,
Life unfolds in silver beams.

Dreams Like Fireflies

Dreams flicker in the darkened night,
Tiny sparks of pure delight.
Like fireflies on a summer's eve,
They dance and weave, they softly leave.

Caught between the stars above,
Whispers of hope, the heart's true love.
Each glow a wish, each flash a chance,
Guiding souls in twilight's dance.

In the quiet, they take flight,
Illuminate the canvas bright.
A symphony of light and grace,
Lost in the moment, a fleeting space.

We chase these dreams, not far behind,
In every shimmer, we seek to find.
A world where wishes freely bloom,
In the glow of night, dispelling gloom.

Celestial Journeys

Across the night, the stars unfold,
Tales of time, in silence told.
Galaxies spin, horizons vast,
Echoes of futures and of the past.

Each twinkle a path, an open door,
Leading our hearts to wander more.
With every wish, we rise and fly,
Touching the place where dreams reside.

Nebulas bloom in colors rare,
Painting the sky with cosmic flair.
Together we drift, in infinite space,
On celestial journeys, we find our place.

The universe calls, with a soft embrace,
Guiding us on through time and space.
In stardust we trust, in light we believe,
Searching for realms that we can weave.

Moonlit Aspirations

Under the moon's soft, silver glow,
We gather dreams, in whispers low.
Each beam a promise, each shadow a quest,
In this night, our hearts find rest.

With stars as guides, our spirits ignite,
Chasing ambitions through the night.
Illuminated paths, in darkness found,
In moonlit aspirations, magic abounds.

The stillness invites, creativity flows,
In quiet moments, inspiration grows.
A canvas painted with gentle light,
Crafting our futures, bold and bright.

With every heartbeat, we soar and dream,
In the embrace of the lunar beam.
Together we rise, hand in hand,
In moonlit aspirations, we boldly stand.

Beyond the Twilight's Gaze

As dusk drapes the world in sighs,
Shadows dance beneath the skies.
Whispers linger, soft and low,
Secrets of the night will flow.

Stars awaken, one by one,
Gracing the realm where day is done.
Moonlight spills on quiet streams,
Guiding us through woven dreams.

The air is thick with tales untold,
Of daring hearts and spirits bold.
Beyond the twilight's gentle fade,
New paths await, unafraid.

In the silence, we can hear,
The echoes of love drawing near.
With every breath, the night we chase,
Together lost in twilight's grace.

Whispers Between the Stars

In the night where silence sings,
Whispers float on fragile wings.
Stars converse in gentle light,
Telling tales of distant flight.

Galaxies woven, vast and bright,
Dance in the canvas of the night.
Cosmic secrets, softly shared,
In the void, we feel they cared.

Every glimmer holds a dream,
Rivers of light, a silver stream.
In their glow, we lose our fears,
Guided home through starlit years.

Between the stars, our wishes play,
Carried on the Milky Way.
We are stardust, we are free,
Whispers of eternity.

Glimmers of Infinite Dreams

Amidst the shadows, softly gleams,
Flickering lights of endless dreams.
Beneath the veil of night's sweet sighs,
Hope takes flight and gently flies.

Visions dance in twilight's glow,
Carving paths where visions flow.
In every heartbeat, every breath,
An echo lives, defying death.

Each glimmer holds a tale to weave,
Of love once lost, of hearts that grieve.
But still we rise, from stardust born,
Together bright, never forlorn.

In every ending, new begins,
A cycle where the light still spins.
Glimmers shine in the darkest night,
Leading us to the dawn's soft light.

Celestial Puzzles and Nightly Queries

In the cosmos, secrets lie,
Beneath the vast and open sky.
Celestial puzzles drift and swirl,
Unraveling like a timeless pearl.

Each star a question, bright and clear,
Glimmers of wisdom, drawing near.
In their glow, we seek and yearn,
For answers in the night, we turn.

The moon, a guide through mysteries,
Breathes softly on our histories.
Echoes whisper through the dark,
Painting dreams with each soft spark.

In the silence, queries bloom,
Ready to lift our hearts from gloom.
Within the night, wonder dwells,
Binding us with invisible spells.

Glimmering Hopes Above

In twilight's embrace we stand,
With wishes whispered to the land.
Each star a beacon, shining bright,
A promise held within the night.

Together we chase what lies ahead,
With laughter shared, our hearts are fed.
Through shadows deep, our dreams will soar,
As glimmering hopes unlock the door.

The sky unfolds its velvet hue,
As starlit paths lead us anew.
In every twinkle, a chance to find,
The courage blossoming in our mind.

So let us dance beneath this dome,
For in our hearts, we are at home.
With glimmering hopes, we'll paint the night,
And chase our dreams 'til morning light.

Silent Prayers Among the Stars

In the quiet of the night, we pray,
The cosmos listen, holding sway.
With every breath, a wish is sown,
Among the stars, we're never alone.

The moonlight bathes our dreams in grace,
As whispers drift through time and space.
Each star a guardian, bright and bold,
Tales of hope and love retold.

We seek the wisdom of the skies,
Where mysteries linger, gently rise.
In silent prayers, our hearts unite,
Guided by stars, we find our light.

As dawn approaches, shadows fade,
The universe, a serenade.
In every moment, faith will guide,
Silent prayers, our souls abide.

A Canvas of Night's Desires

The night unfolds its canvas wide,
Where dreams and wishes gently bide.
With every stroke, a story told,
In hues of blue and threads of gold.

In shadows deep, our hopes reside,
Painted with longing, side by side.
The stars above, they twinkle bright,
Illuminating our deepest flight.

With whispers soft, we call the muse,
To spark the fire we wish to use.
Each color bends, a tale to weave,
In night's embrace, we learn to believe.

The canvas wakes as dawn draws near,
Yet in our hearts, the night is clear.
With desires bold, we leave our mark,
In every stroke, igniting spark.

Celestial Ballet of Dreams

In the night sky, dreams intertwine,
A ballet of stars, so divine.
Each twirl and leap, a wish set free,
The cosmos dance in harmony.

With every pulse, the galaxies sway,
Guiding us gently on our way.
In cosmic rhythms, our hopes align,
A celestial waltz, our hearts enshrined.

As planets glide on pathways vast,
We chase the shadows of our past.
In this ballet, we find our place,
With every movement, a touch of grace.

So let us dance beneath the stars,
With open hearts, we'll travel far.
In the celestial ballet, we belong,
Together we sing our timeless song.

The Dance of Night's Wishes

In shadows deep, the wishes weave,
Beneath the stars, our hearts believe.
With every twirl, the night unfolds,
Embracing dreams that fate beholds.

The moonlight casts a silver glow,
As whispers rise from below.
In twilight's hush, the secrets gleam,
We dance together, lost in dream.

Each twinkling light a hope reborn,
In gentle night, we're never torn.
With every step, our souls align,
In this sweet moment, love's design.

As time drifts on like gentle stream,
The dance persists, a cherished theme.
Through night's embrace, our wishes glide,
Together, love, we'll turn the tide.

Stardust Diaries of the Heart

In pages torn, our stories lie,
Written in stars that fill the sky.
Each heartbeat echoes, whispers loud,
Stardust dreams, amidst the crowd.

Through realms of night, our voices blend,
In cosmic scripts, our love transcends.
With every breath, we write anew,
A diary of moments, just us two.

The luminescence guides our way,
In silvered glows, we laugh and play.
A tapestry of hopes and fears,
In stardust ink, we trace the years.

As we turn pages, day by day,
In sacred words, our hearts will stay.
With every chapter, time we chart,
These stardust diaries of the heart.

Skylit Dreams this Evening

The evening brings a canvas wide,
With stars like dreams that gently guide.
In twilight's breath, we find our truth,
Awakening the heart of youth.

Soft whispers sail on night's cool breeze,
Carried high through the swaying trees.
As shadows dance upon the ground,
In starlit dreams, the lost are found.

With each soft glow, our hopes take flight,
Illuminating the quiet night.
Together, love, we chase the gleam,
In the warm embrace of a shared dream.

This evening holds a world of light,
In skylit dreams, we feel just right.
As stars wink down, our spirits soar,
In this sweet moment, we crave more.

Glimpse of a Starlit Tomorrow

With every dawn, a new chance grows,
Like sunflowers turning to the glow.
In starlit paths, our journey starts,
With whispers soft, and open hearts.

Tomorrow's dreams, on wings they rise,
Reflecting hopes in endless skies.
Through gentle night, we wander free,
As constellations call to thee.

A glimpse of love in twilight's grasp,
Together tight, in fate we clasp.
With every star, a promise made,
In the night's embrace, we won't fade.

So let us tread where shadows play,
With every step, we find our way.
In starlit glow, our futures gleam,
A vibrant dance, a hopeful dream.

Celestial Echoes of Forgotten Dreams

In stillness, the stars softly sigh,
Whispers of past we dare not deny.
Ghosts of wishes that twinkled and played,
Fleeting visions in twilight displayed.

A dance of shadows, a flickering light,
Casting reflections on the velvet night.
Each echo a promise, a secret untold,
In the heart of the cosmos, our stories unfold.

Linger in silence, let memories stream,
As comets streak by with a distant gleam.
A tapestry woven from stardust and time,
In heaven's embrace, we silently climb.

Fallen dreams linger where silence will reign,
Their essence persists in the cosmic domain.
With every heartbeat, a wish takes its flight,
Celestial murmurs cradle the night.

Nostalgic Whispers of the Night Sky

Beneath the vast dome, my soul takes wing,
Every twinkle a tale of what love could bring.
Echoes of laughter float soft in the air,
Nostalgic moments that dance without care.

The moon hums a tune, tender and slow,
While shadows remember what we used to know.
Stardust and memories weave through the dark,
Painting the sky with a luminous spark.

Cool breezes carry a soft, sweet refrain,
Recollections awaken, like drops of warm rain.
The night sky a canvas, so rich and so deep,
Nestled in starlight, our promises keep.

Lost in the cosmos, I breathe in the night,
Awash in the glow of dreams taking flight.
With each gust of wind, I feel you near,
Whispers of love that I long to hear.

Dreams Under the Ethereal Glow

Under the blanket of shimmering light,
Fantasies dance, tender and bright.
The veil of the cosmos, a shimmering seam,
Enfolding our wishes in the fabric of dream.

Soft pastel shades paint the edges of dark,
A symphony plays, each note a soft spark.
As night gently hums a lullaby sweet,
A mosaic of dreams beneath stars we meet.

Echoes of passion entwined in the air,
Drifting like wisps of a silken prayer.
The warmth of the heavens, the chill of the night,
Embrace us in whispers, celestial delight.

In this delicate moment where time feels so slow,
We gather the fragments of all that we know.
Beneath the ethereal glow, hearts intertwine,
In dreams we find solace, a love so divine.

Songs from the Edge of the Universe

From galaxies far, a melody calls,
Rustling through stardust, a symphony falls.
Notes drift like comets across cosmic seas,
Resonating softly in the celestial breeze.

Each chord a journey through time and space,
Gentle reminders of a lost embrace.
Harmonies ripple through shadows and light,
Songs from the edge of the universe bright.

Whispers of planets and secrets untold,
In the fabric of night, our dreams we uphold.
The rhythm of orbits, a dance so profound,
In the silence of cosmos, our hearts are unbound.

United we stand, on this fragile blue sphere,
With echoes of song we long to hold dear.
As stardust surrounds us, we endlessly sway,
In songs from the universe, forever we'll stay.

The Magic of Distant Gleams

Stars twinkle softly, a brush of light,
Painting the sky with the dreams of night.
Whispers of time in the cosmic flow,
Secrets scattered, where stardust grows.

Galaxies swirl in a dance of grace,
Infinite wonders, a vast embrace.
Through the darkness, hope finds a way,
Guiding the lost, come what may.

Radiant visions in the twilight gleam,
Awakening hearts, igniting a dream.
With every flicker, a story unfolds,
Of love and laughter, of courage bold.

In the silence, find the glow within,
For even in shadows, the light can begin.
The magic of distant gleams shall ignite,
Our spirits forever, in the velvet night.

Heartbeats Under Cosmic Canopies

Beneath the stars, heartbeats resound,
In the embrace of night, we are found.
Each pulse a whisper, a song of the soul,
Echoing softly, making us whole.

Through branches of starlight, our dreams take flight,
Under cosmic canopies, we dance with delight.
With every heartbeat, the universe sings,
Connecting our essence to all living things.

Time drifts like stardust in the cool night air,
Moments unfold with a magical flair.
We are stardust children, woven in grace,
Finding our rhythm in this infinite space.

Together we wander, lost in the glow,
With hearts intertwined, in the cosmic flow.
Here under canopies, where wishes ignite,
We celebrate life in the depths of the night.

Reveries in a Nebula

In a nebula's embrace, dreams softly sway,
Colors of twilight merge into the gray.
Whispers of starlight guide our way,
In reveries born from the night and the day.

Floating through nebulae, our spirits drift,
Lost in the beauty, the purest gift.
Each shimmer a promise, each glow a kiss,
A dance of light in a cosmic bliss.

We craft our visions from the wisps of time,
Each thought a star, each feeling a rhyme.
Together we wander through shadows and beams,
Collecting these fragments of luminous dreams.

As the universe breathes, we find our refrain,
In the vastness we gather, and never complain.
For in every whisper, the cosmos does sing,
Of reveries cherished, love's radiant spring.

The Lullaby of Glittering Orbs

The night hums softly, a lullaby sweet,
As glittering orbs spin in rhythmic feet.
They waltz through the sky, a mesmerizing trance,
Inviting our hearts to join in the dance.

With each tender glimmer, we find our peace,
In the symphony of stars, worries release.
A chorus of light, a gentle embrace,
Wraps us in magic, a warm, sacred space.

Underneath the canopy of the endless night,
Glittering orbs cast their silvery light.
They whisper of dreams in a language divine,
Weaving together the threads of time.

As we drift to slumber, our spirits take flight,
Carried by the lullaby of celestial light.
In the arms of the cosmos, we rest and renew,
Awakening tomorrow, with the skies painted blue.

Milton Keynes UK
Ingram Content Group UK Ltd.
UKHW021928011224
451790UK00005B/56